D1366925

Marion Public Library
1095 6th Avenue
Marion, IA 52302-3428
(319) 377-3412

HOW DOES THE WIND BLOW?

PATRICIA J. MURPHY

Marshall Cavendish
Benchmark
New York

To Olivia—Here's to our next WINDSDAY celebration! With love, Auntie P.

The author thanks Doug Sanders, her editor, and Dennis R. Cain, National Weather Service meteorologist and "Professor Weather," for their assistance in her windy work.

Marshall Cavendish Benchmark
99 White Plains Road
Tarrytown, New York 10591-9001
www.marshallcavendish.us

All Web sites were available and accurate when this book was sent to press.

Editor: D. Sanders
Editorial Director: Michelle Bisson
Art Director: Anahid Hamparian
Series Designer: Alex Ferrari

Library of Congress Cataloging-in-Publication Data

Murphy, Patricia J., 1963–
How does the wind blow? / by Patricia J. Murphy.
p. cm. — (Tell me why, tell me how)
Summary: "An examination of the phenomena and scientific principles behind wind"—Provided by publisher.
Includes bibliographical references and index.
ISBN-13: 978-0-7614-2107-8
ISBN-10: 0-7614-2107-6
1. Winds—Juvenile literature. I. Title. II. Series.

QC931.4.M87 2006
551.51'8—dc22

2005016475

Photo research by Candlepants Incorporated

Cover photo: Julie Habel/Corbis

The photographs in this book are used by permission and through the courtesy of: *Getty Images:* Tony Hutchings, 1. *Peter Arnold Inc.:* K. Shindel/UNEP, 4. *Photo Researchers Inc.:* Lynwood M. Chase, 5; Richard Hutchings, 6; NASA, 12; James Stevenson, 19. *Corbis:* Phil Banko, 7; John McAnulty, 8; Joson/zefa, 9; Dennis Cooper/zefa, 14; Frithjof Hiirdes/zefa, 16; Warren Faidley, 15; Jim Zuckerman, 18; Bettmann, 20, 22; Tony Aruza, 23; Lafi, 24; Roy Morsch/zefa, 25. *SuperStock:* age footstock, 10; Comstock, 11. *Veer:* Jim Barber, 17.

Printed in Malaysia
1 3 5 6 4 2

CONTENTS

The wind powers windmills,
big and small.

What Is the Wind?

Wind is air that is in motion. Tiny particles called air **molecules** move up and down and all around. These busy particles can move fast or slowly. They can travel over mountains, oceans, and miles and miles of land. When these particles move from side to side, wind is the result.

It is the wind that blows hats off people's heads and makes the grass sway. It is also the wind that scatters piles of autumn leaves and carries a balloon far away. Trees, flowers, and plants count on wind in order to move their seeds from place to place. Birds, insects, and

Many plants need wind to scatter or move their seeds.

5

butterflies need wind to fly and flutter around. People use wind to fly airplanes and kites—and to power windmills. But wind's most important job is to bring us the **weather**.

Will it be cloudy, stormy, or clear tomorrow? The answer is in the wind. It is the wind that carries clouds and storms that create changes in Earth's **atmosphere.** These daily changes (also called weather) affect what you wear each day.

Storms bring strong winds. Watch out!

They also affect whether you stay inside or go outside. Sometimes, they even affect how you feel.

The wind is invisible. So, sometimes you hardly even know it is there. But even when the wind is calm, you can feel it. Hold your hand in front of your mouth. Then take a

breath and blow it out. Or fan your face with your hand. What you have just felt is wind.

On Earth we can also feel changes in **air pressure.** Air pressure is the weight of the air pushing down on an object. Changes in air pressure mean changes in the weather. That is when the wind really starts to blow.

Now I Know!

How does the wind help plants and trees?

It scatters their seeds.

Take in a deep breath, then blow it out. You have just made a little bit of wind.

The Chinook wind helps to melt this snowy scene.

What Kinds of Winds Are There?

Some winds are named for the directions they come from. The north wind and west wind are two examples. Others are named for the places where they occur. The hot, dry Santa Ana winds blow through the Santa Ana Mountains in California. The Chinook wind gets its name from the Native American word meaning "snow eater." This wind quickly eats—or melts—snow.

Long ago, people gave the winds names and human qualities.

California's Santa Ana winds help this windsurfer to fly.

9

Some believed that winds had magical powers or were actual gods swirling above them. Others thought that wind came from a crack in the Earth or a hole in a mountain. Many made up stories to explain the winds' force and power. As people traveled to new places in the world, they noticed patterns in the wind. They soon used these patterns to travel more quickly and easily.

Sailors use the wind to help them get where they need to go.

In the polar regions, polar easterlies blow from east to west. Elsewhere on Earth, the westerlies—winds coming from the west—move weather systems from west to east.

The trade winds gust and blow near the equator.

Near the **equator** in the tropical regions, northeast and southeast trade winds blow from the east. Early sailors found that the trade winds helped speed them on their way when they had goods to trade, so that is how the winds got their name. On the return trip home, the force of the westerlies often made for a quick journey.

The northeast and southeast trade winds meet at an area along the equator. This region is where Earth's tropical rain forests grow. It is also the place where the storms that later

The jet stream is a river of winds that travels through the atmosphere.

become hurricanes begin. There the trade winds cause air to rise and rain to fall. With its steady rain and slight wind, the area is called the Doldrums—an old English word that means "dull."

Between the trade winds and the westerlies are the horse latitudes. There the winds blow out and away from the area. This motion is set off by pockets of high air pressure. These pockets cause light winds. With such little wind, early traders had to dump heavy loads (including their horses at times) overboard to get moving.

These are some of the wind patterns that are at work around the globe and in your own backyard. Depending on where you live, you may feel breezes blowing off water, around mountains, or through valleys. You might also feel the effects of upper atmosphere winds called the **jet stream.** Whatever the weather is around you, you can be sure that the jet stream has something to do with it. The jet stream helps direct and build all types of weather all over the planet.

Now I Know!

In what part of the world are the trade winds found?

Near the equator.

Winds can gust
with great speed.

How Fast Does the Wind Blow?

Winds can blow as gently as a few miles per hour. They can also gust with great speed. In the form of a hurricane, winds can race by at more than 100 miles (161 kilometers) per hour. What makes the wind blow either fast or slowly? It is a special force that is caused by the differences in air pressure in a given area. Scientists say it is this force that "drives the wind." The greater the difference between a patch of high air pressure and low air pressure, the faster the wind will blow.

To predict wind speed, meteorologists first chart areas of high and low pressure on

Knowing the wind's speed and direction can help meteorologists forecast harsh weather, such as this thunderstorm.

15

weather maps. They do this by connecting the areas, or dots, of equal air pressures to form a line. This line is called an **isobar.** The closer together the isobars are on a map, the faster the wind will blow in those areas. The farther apart the isobars are, the slower the wind will be.

To measure wind speed, meteorologists use a tool called an **anemometer.** Most anemometers have cups that spin as the winds blow. Anemometers are connected to machines that keep track of the number of spins in a given period of time. The machines use the number of spins to figure out the speed of the wind.

Meteorologists use a **wind vane**

Meteorologists use weather maps to predict wind speed.

to record the wind's direction. A wind vane has an arrow and is marked with four compass directions—north, south, east, and west. As the wind blows, the arrow points to the direction that the wind is blowing from.

Now I Know!
What does an anemometer measure?

Wind speed.

Knowing the wind's speed and direction helps meteorologists predict weather changes. These readings give clues as to what type of weather is coming and how soon it might arrive. This information is important when there is a chance of severe weather. Thunderstorms, tornadoes, and hurricanes often travel quickly and cause a lot of harm. An accurate forecast can give you enough time to get to a safe place.

Meteorologists use wind vanes (also called weather vanes) to figure out the wind's direction.

Tornadoes can cause
great damage.

When Can the Wind Be Harmful?

By itself, the wind is rarely harmful. But when it starts picking things up and blowing them around, it can cause great harm.

Often, winds play a big part in harsh weather. Thunderstorms, tornadoes, or hurricanes all come with high winds. Thunderstorms bring heavy rains, dangerous winds, (up to 75 miles or 121 kilometers per hour), thunder, and lightning. Tornadoes come from thunderstorms. First a column of warm air that rises up through a thunderstorm begins to spin. The faster the air rises, the faster it spins. This movement then causes cooler air to sink and the tornado's powerful winds to blow and blow.

Trees bend and shake when a strong wind is blowing.

A man braces himself against a powerful hurricane.

When a tornado touches the ground, it can last a few minutes or as long as an hour. No matter how long a tornado stays, its damaging winds can rip trees out of the ground, push trains off their tracks, and tear apart entire towns. A tornado's whipping winds can reach up to 300 miles (483 kilometers) per hour.

Nearly 75 percent of all tornadoes, about 1,000 each year, touch down in the central United States. Areas of high and low pressure often meet there. These pressures then form the thunderstorms that turn into tornadoes. The part of the country stretching from Texas to Minnesota is called Tornado Alley. It has more tornadoes than any other place on Earth.

20

Along the coasts of the Atlantic, Pacific, and Indian oceans, hurricanes rule. Winds blow these dangerous tropical storms over ocean waters and nearby shores. Hurricanes begin as groups of showers and thunderstorms that gather over warm parts of the ocean.

Now I Know!
What is the calm center of a hurricane called?

The eye.

These storms come together from different directions to form a hurricane. A hurricane lifts warm air and ocean water upward. Often violent, a hurricane gets its circular motion from the Earth's **rotation.** As the Earth spins, so does the hurricane. The center, or eye, of the storm is calm and quiet. But the rotating air around the eye can cause the deadliest winds.

Whether it is a powerful hurricane or a gentle autumn breeze, wind is the Earth's way of trying to balance temperatures. But, since the Earth has a wide range of different temperatures, this balance will never happen. This is a good thing. Without differences in temperatures, the weather would be the same every day—and everywhere. The seasons would never change, and there would be no wind.

Wind blows because the Earth is
unevenly heated by the Sun.

How Does the Wind Blow?

Wind cannot move by itself. It takes the Sun to get it going. Because of Earth's shape and rotation, the Sun does not heat our planet evenly. This leaves some parts of Earth, such as the North and South poles, cold. Other areas, near the equator for example, are hot. Earth's different temperatures cause the atmosphere's air pressure to be different from place to place. The differences in the air pressure cause the air to move from side to side across the land and water. Wind is what we call this moving air.

The wind is nature's way of trying to balance the different air pressures found on Earth.

How exactly does the wind blow? Think of it as a dance between warm and cold air molecules. The warmer, lighter air molecules begin to rise. This creates low air pressure. These molecules then expand or spread out. As the warm air rises and expands, cooler air and high pressure move in and fill the space that the warm air leaves behind. This constant flow of hot and cold air is the Earth's way of trying to balance the differences in air pressure that the various temperatures cause.

As the wind blows, it speeds up over water and slows down over land. Cooler water temperatures push the warmer molecules higher and higher. Over land, the air molecules bump into hills, mountains, and other landforms. A force called **friction** slows them

The wind is always blowing somewhere.

24

down. But winds never lose their speed for long. They never stop, because the temperatures on Earth are never balanced. So the wind keeps blowing and blowing twenty-four hours a day, seven days a week.

When wind travels, it never moves in a straight line. This is because of the Earth's **rotation.** As the Earth rotates or spins on its **axis,** the poles move more slowly than the area near the equator. This causes the winds in the Northern **Hemisphere** to turn

Without wind, we couldn't fly kites.

25

to the right as they approach the North Pole. In the Southern Hemisphere, the winds move to the left. This is called the Coriolis effect.

No matter what direction they are blowing in, we live in a world of winds. These currents of air blow through Earth's atmosphere like rivers flow into the ocean.

Activity

MAKE A WIND VANE

A wind vane is also often called a weather vane. Create your own version of the world's first weather tool. It will tell you where the wind is coming from.

What You Will Need
a piece of cardboard, about 8½ by 11 inches
a pencil
scissors
a water bottle
modeling clay
a pie pan or other flat aluminum pan
a few small rocks
a compass
a marker
a pen

How to Make It
1. Draw an arrow on a piece of cardboard with a pencil. Make a mark midway down its length. Cut the arrow out with the scissors.
2. Attach the arrow to the top of the straw at the arrow's midpoint (or middle).

3. Place the arrow and straw into an empty water bottle with the straw going down into the bottle, as if you were going to drink the water with the straw.

4. Use a small piece of modeling clay to attach the bottom of the bottle to the middle of the pie pan or aluminum container. Put a couple of rocks around the bottom of the bottle in the container, to hold your wind vane down.

5. Use a compass and marker to mark the four directions (North, South, East, and West) on the outer edge of the pie pan or aluminum container with a ballpoint pen.

6. Stand back and watch the wind blow!

7. Remember that the direction your wind vane points to is the direction the wind is blowing from. If your arrow is pointing to the north, the wind is blowing from the north. This wind is called the north wind.

How to Use It

1. Observe wind directions daily to see where the wind is blowing from.

2. Record your observations in a special notebook or journal.

3. Make and compare daily, weekly, or monthly readings to see how and when the direction of the wind changes.

4. Share your notes with others.

5. Make other weather tools to create a full-service weather station.

Glossary

air pressure—The weight of the air pressing down on Earth.

anemometer—An instrument that measures the speed of the wind. It has three or four cups that spin around as the wind blows.

atmosphere—The air surrounding the Earth. It is made up of many different substances including nitrogen, oxygen, other gases, water vapor, and tiny particles. The atmosphere has five layers: the troposphere, stratosphere, mesosphere, thermosphere, and exosphere.

axis—An imaginary straight line that passes through an object and around which the object spins. Earth's axis passes between its North and South poles.

equator—An imaginary line around Earth halfway between the North and South poles. It divides the earth into two halves—the Northern Hemisphere and the Southern Hemisphere.

friction—The force that tends to stop an object from moving.

gravity—The force that pulls objects toward Earth. This force also keeps the planets in orbit spinning around the Sun.

hemisphere—One half of Earth. The Northern Hemisphere is Earth's northern half. The Southern Hemisphere is its southern half.

isobar—A line on a weather map that connects places with the same levels of air pressure.

jet stream—A high-speed "river" of air that blows from the west to east very high in the atmosphere. It helps airplanes traveling east fly at faster speeds.

molecule—A group of atoms. An atom is the smallest piece of matter that can be divided.

poles—The North and South poles are found at the ends of the axis that the Earth spins around.

rotation—The act of spinning around a central point or axis.

weather—The changing condition of the atmosphere including the temperature, air pressure, humidity, winds, clouds, and rainfall or snowfall amounts.

wind vane—A weather tool that tells where the wind is coming from. It is also called a weather vane.

Find Out More

BOOKS

Bauer, Marion Dane. *Wind*. New York: Aladdin, 2003.

Cobb, Vicki. *I Face the Wind*. New York: HarperCollins, 2003.

Cooper, Jason. *Wind*. Vero Beach, FL: Rourke, 2003.

Flanagan, Alice K. *Wind*. Chanhassen, MN: Child's World, 2003.

Frost, Helen. *Wind*. Mankato, MN: Capstone, 2004.

Sievert, Terri. *Wind*. Mankato, MN: Capstone, 2005.

Williams, Judith. *Why Is It Windy?* Berkeley Heights, NJ: Enslow, 2005.

WEB SITES

National Oceanic and Atmospheric Administration
http://www.noaa.gov
The official Web site of the NOAA offers information on weather, oceans, satellites, climate, coasts, charting and navigation, fisheries, and more.

National Weather Service
http://www.nws.noaa.gov
The Office of the National Weather Service offers weather warnings, observations, models, weather safety, and an information center.

National Weather Service: Jetstream
http://www.srh.noaa.gov/srh/jetstream
The online weather school from the National Weather Service offers information on a variety of weather topics including the atmosphere, meteorology, global weather, and storms.

The Weather Channel
http://www.weather.com
Offers up-to-the-minute weather reports, Doppler radar and satellite images, current temperatures, and a hurricane central.

WW2010: The Weather World 2010 Project
http://WW2010.atmos.uiuc.edu/(Gh)/home.rxml
This weather project from the University of Illinois includes information on meteorology, projects and activities, and resources and curriculum.

Index

Page numbers for illustrations are in **boldface.**

240577611